My Family Tree Book

by Sam Hutchinson
and Catherine Bruzzone
illustrated by Franziska Höllbacher

b small publishing
www.bsmall.co.uk

What is a family tree?

Your family tree is the map of **your** family. It shows how you are related, or joined, to the other people in your family — just like the branches and twigs are joined to the trunk of a tree.

The picture opposite shows a common family tree. Can you see the lines joining the sister, parents and grandparents? These lines show how they are **related**. These people are **relations**.

This may not look like your family. Perhaps you have more or fewer brothers or sisters. You may have aunts and uncles and lots of cousins. You may think of some of your friends as your family. Family trees can show all these people. They can also give you many fascinating facts, like when your parent or parents were born, how many brothers and sisters a grandparent has, or how old a grandparent was when they died. Families are all different.

You will be able to draw your own family tree at the end of this book. Families come in all shapes and sizes and we show some exciting and different trees later on pages 22 to 29. But before you do, discover as much as you can about your family on the next pages. You won't fill in all the spaces - or you might need extra paper for even more answers. This is your family.

You may find much more information or photos than you have room for on these pages. Clip extra paper on to the pages.

You could make a separate book with the extra pages. Punch holes in the edges and thread through pieces of wool to hold them together.

Cut photos to fit the spaces provided.

To make a special pocket out of the back cover, cut a triangle from card and glue or tape it to the bottom right of a page or inside the front cover.

This is a family tree very much like the author's. And remember, every family is different, so you will probably leave some bits blank when you make your family tree.

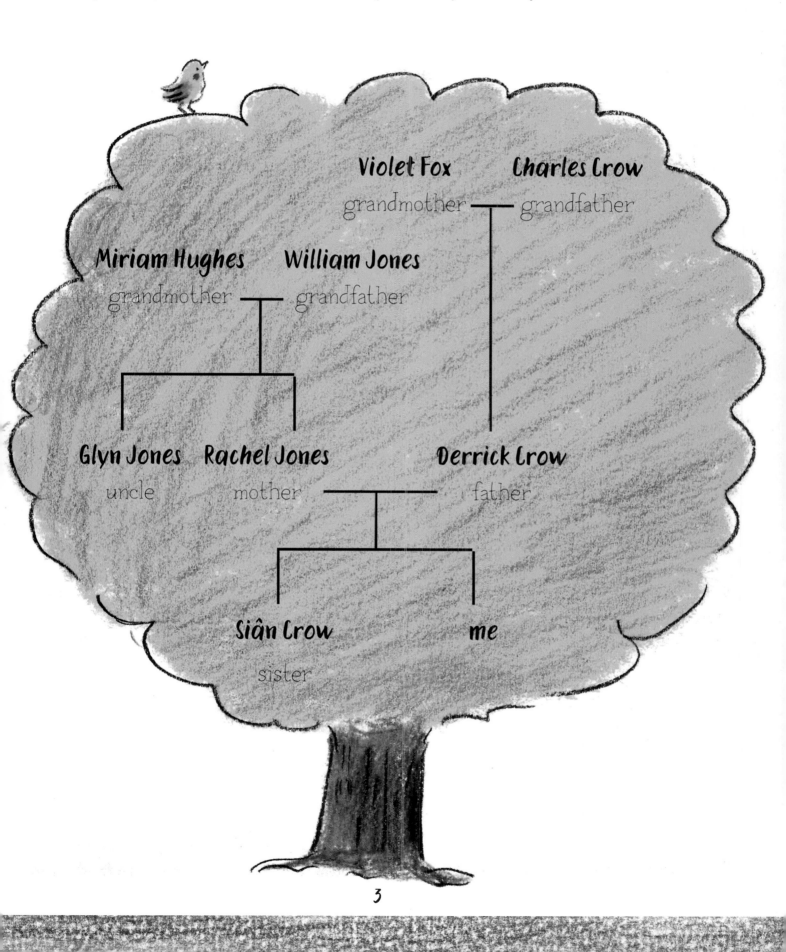

Violet Fox
grandmother

Charles Crow
grandfather

Miriam Hughes
grandmother

William Jones
grandfather

Glyn Jones
uncle

Rachel Jones
mother

Derrick Crow
father

Siân Crow
sister

me

All about me

My birthday

_____

Year I was born

_____

Where I was born

_____

My earliest recorded weight

_____

Day of the week I was born

_____

Names of my parent or parents

_____

Names of any brothers

_____

Names of any sisters

_____

Name of person who looks after me

_____

Stick in a photograph.

First photo of me

Stick in a photograph.

Me, age . . . .

My name is _____

Other people who live with me

_____

Where I live now

_____

Telephone number

_____

Languages I can speak

_____

Names of schools or playgroups

_____

Fill this space with more about yourself or draw a self-portrait.

My parent or parents

These next four pages are where you can collect information about *your* parent or parents. Every family is different so use these four pages to discover your family. Maybe you only have one parent? Or you have a mum and a dad? Or two mums? Perhaps you have an adoptive parent and a birth parent? Take extra sheets of paper if you need them and clip them into the book. And remember, you won't be filling in all the information – this is your family.

I call them

_____

Their birthday

_____

Year they were born

_____

Where they were born

_____

They have ____ sisters

They have ____ brothers

Names of any brothers

_____

Names of any sisters

_____

Names of schools they went to

_____

Stick in a photograph.

My . . . . , age . . .

Stick in a photograph.

My . . . . , age . . .

Their full name is _____

A memory from their school days

....

....

....

Favourite colour

....

Favourite food

....

Can you find their school or college certificates? Did they do gymnastics, science activities or chess club?

Jobs

....

Their age when
I was born

....

Colour of their hair

....

Colour of their eyes

....

Draw your parent here.

7

My parent

If you have more than one parent, write about them here. If you have one parent, draw a picture of you together and attach it to this page.

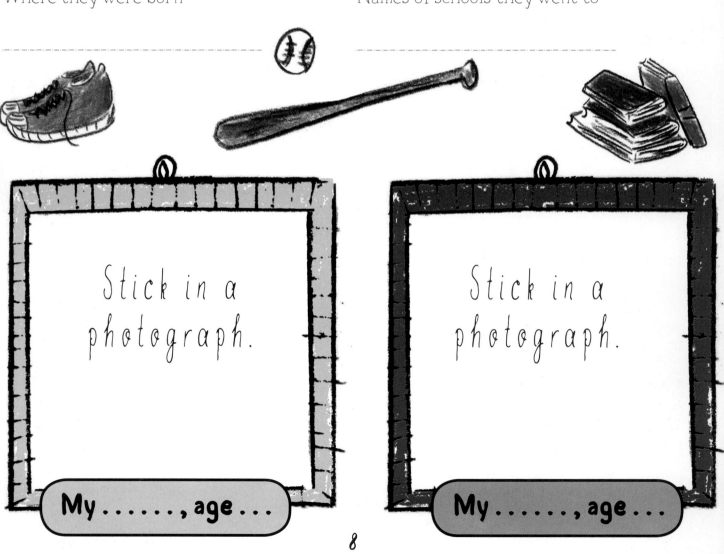

I call them

_____

Their birthday

_____

Year they were born

_____

Where they were born

_____

They have _____ sisters

They have _____ brothers

Names of any brothers

_____

Names of any sisters

_____

Names of schools they went to

_____

Stick in a photograph.

My . . . . . . , age . . .

Stick in a photograph.

My . . . . . . , age . . .

Their full name is _____

A memory from their school days

Can you find their school or college certificates? Did they do gymnastics, science activities or chess club?

Jobs

Their age when
I was born

Colour of their hair

Colour of their eyes

Favourite colour

Favourite food

Draw your parent here.

9

My sisters and brothers

If you do not have any brothers or sisters, put 'O' in the boxes below. Stick a drawing of your family over this page. Or write about an imaginary brother or sister.

Number of sisters

Number of brothers

My oldest sister or brother is called

Date she or he was born

Where she or he was born

My next oldest sister or brother is called

Date she or he was born

Where she or he was born

My next oldest sister or brother is called

Date she or he was born

Where she or he was born

If you have more than three sisters and brothers, write their details on a piece of paper and clip it to this page. Some of your sisters or brothers might be step- or half-sisters or brothers. If you want to you can write more details about them or how you are related to them:

"Rose is my half-sister.
She and I have the same father."

"Robert is my stepbrother. He is John's son. John lives with my mother."

Stick in a
photograph.

My . . . . , age . . . .

Stick in a
photograph.

My . . . . , age . . . .

Who is in each photo? How old are they? Where were the photos taken? When were they taken?

11

My aunts and uncles

Aunts and uncles are your parent's sisters and brothers.
If your parent doesn't have any sisters or brothers, write
about other adults who spend a lot of time with your family.

Related to or friends with my ....

Name	Name ....
Date she or he was born	Date she or he was born
....	....
Where she or he was born	Where she or he was born
....	....
Where he or she lives now	Where he or she lives now
....	....
Person he or she lives with	Person he or she lives with
....	....
Names of children	Names of children
....	....

Your aunts' or uncles'
children are your
cousins. You can fill
in more detail about them
on pages 16 and 17.

Name ....

Date she or he was born

....

Where she or he was born

....

Where he or she lives now

....

Person he or she lives with

....

Names of children

....

If your parent has more than three sisters and brothers, write their details on a piece of paper and clip it here. Can you find a photo of them all together as children?

Stick in a photograph.

Stick in a photograph.

....

Write the names of the people in each photo. Where were the photos taken? When were they taken? Do you have a photo of the same people now?

....

More of my aunts and uncles

Related to or friends with my ....

Name ....   Name ....

Date she or he was born   Date she or he was born

....

Where she or he was born   Where she or he was born

....

Where he or she lives now   Where he or she lives now

....

Person he or she lives with   Person he or she lives with

....

Names of children   Names of children

....

....

Your aunts' or uncles' children are your *cousins*. You can fill in more detail about them on pages 16 and 17.

14

Name _____

Date she or he was born

_____

Where she or he was born

_____

Where he or she lives now

_____

Person he or she lives with

_____

Names of children

_____

_____

If your parent has more than three sisters and brothers, write their details on a piece of paper and clip it here. Can you find a photo of them all together as children?

Stick in a photograph.

Stick in a photograph.

_____

_____

Write the names of the people in each photo. Where were the photos taken? When were they taken? Do you have a photo of the same people now?

My cousins

Some families use the word 'cousin' for the children of your parents' sisters and brothers. Some families use the word 'cousin' for other relatives as well, or even very close family friends.

If your parent comes from a large family, you may have lots of cousins! First put their oldest brother or sister's name and then fill in the details for each cousin.

Name of oldest cousin

Their parents' names

Date and place she or he was born

What we do together

Name of next oldest cousin

Their parents' names

Date and place she or he was born

What we do together

More of my cousins

Paste a photo of your cousins on a sheet of paper. Under it, write their names and how old they are.

Name of oldest cousin	Name of next oldest cousin
-----	-----
Their parents' names	Their parents' names
-----	-----
-----	-----
Date and place she or he was born	Date and place she or he was born
-----	-----
What we do together	What we do together
-----	-----
-----	-----

If you don't have a photo of your cousins, draw a picture of them. Which of your cousins is the tallest and which is the smallest?

My grandparent

The people on this page looked after my

_____

Their name is

_____

Grandparents are your parents' parents, or the people who looked after your parents. If your grandparents are no longer alive, you may need to do some detective work to fill in these pages. Can your parents help?

Name I call them

_____

Date they were born

_____

Where they were born

_____

Name of school

_____

Names of any sisters

_____

Names of any brothers

_____

Jobs

_____

Age when my mother or father was born

_____

Something they remember from the past

_____

_____

Stick in a photograph.

My grandparent, age . . .

My grandparent

Their name is

Name of school

Name I call them

Jobs

Date they were born

Age when my mother or father was born

Where they were born

Something they remember from the past

Names of any sisters

Names of any brothers

Stick in a photograph.

My grandparent, age . . .

Ask about the things that were different when your grandparents were young. What style of clothes did they wear? What games did they play? Can they remember something important in the news? Why not make a book or an audio recording of their memories?

My grandparent

The people on this page looked after my

....

Their name is

....

....

Name I call them

....

Date they were born

....

Where they were born

....

Name of school

....

If your grandparents are no longer alive, you may need to do some detective work to fill in these pages. Can your parents help? Or your aunts and uncles?

Names of any sisters

....

Names of any brothers

....

Jobs

....

Age when my mother or father was born

....

Something they remember from the past

....

....

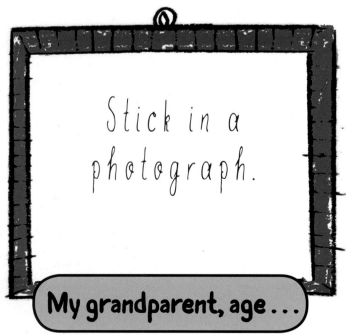

Stick in a photograph.

My grandparent, age . . .

My grandparent

Their name is

_____

Name I call them

_____

Date they were born

_____

Where they were born

_____

Names of any sisters

_____

Names of any brothers

_____

Name of school

_____

Jobs

_____

Age when my mother or father was born

_____

Something they remember from the past

_____

_____

Stick in a photograph.

My grandparent, age . . .

Do any of your grandparents have a marriage certificate? It will show you when and where they were married. If not, ask them about their first home.

Family groups

Many family tree designs look like actual trees with you at the bottom and your family making up the branches above.

Since all families are unique, you can sometimes make small trees with only a few branches. Or you might have huge trees with lots of branches. A big tree is very hard to draw and might not work for your family.

Start by putting the important people in your life into different 'Family Groups'. Look at the example on the opposite page.

Remember, this is *your* family and you might not be able to fill in every group.

22

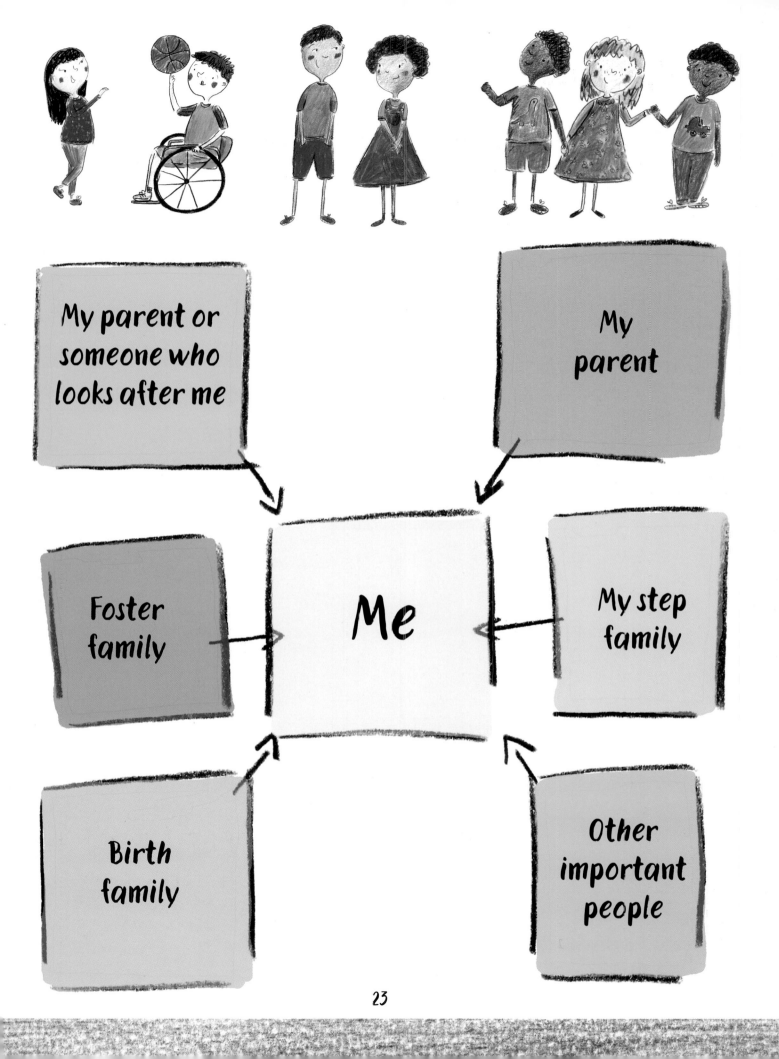

My parent or someone who looks after me

My parent

Foster family

Me

My step family

Birth family

Other important people

23

My own family tree

Fill in your own family tree here.

To start with, do a simple one – just any sisters and brothers, any parents and grandparents. For brothers and sisters, put the eldest on your left and the younger ones on your right. (Look at the tree on page 3 as a guide.)

If you want, ask someone to help you make a larger tree. This could show aunts and uncles, cousins, and perhaps grandparents' brothers and sisters – or even great-grandparents! You could add more details to your tree, like:

b. = born
m. = married
d. = died

Granny Black
b. 1 June 1923
Swansea

Turn over and look at the following ideas for family trees if this design does not work for you.

See instructions for tracing on page 26. Cut cut and colour in faces for your tree from page 31.

Full family wheel

This family wheel might suit your family better than the tree on page 25.

Change the different sections of the wheel so that you can include all of the people in your family.

To create your own family wheel, place a piece of tracing paper over the template. Hold steady and draw around the shape. Turn the tracing paper over and scribble over the lines with a soft pencil. Turn over again and tape on to paper or card. Retrace firmly over the original lines. Remove tracing paper.

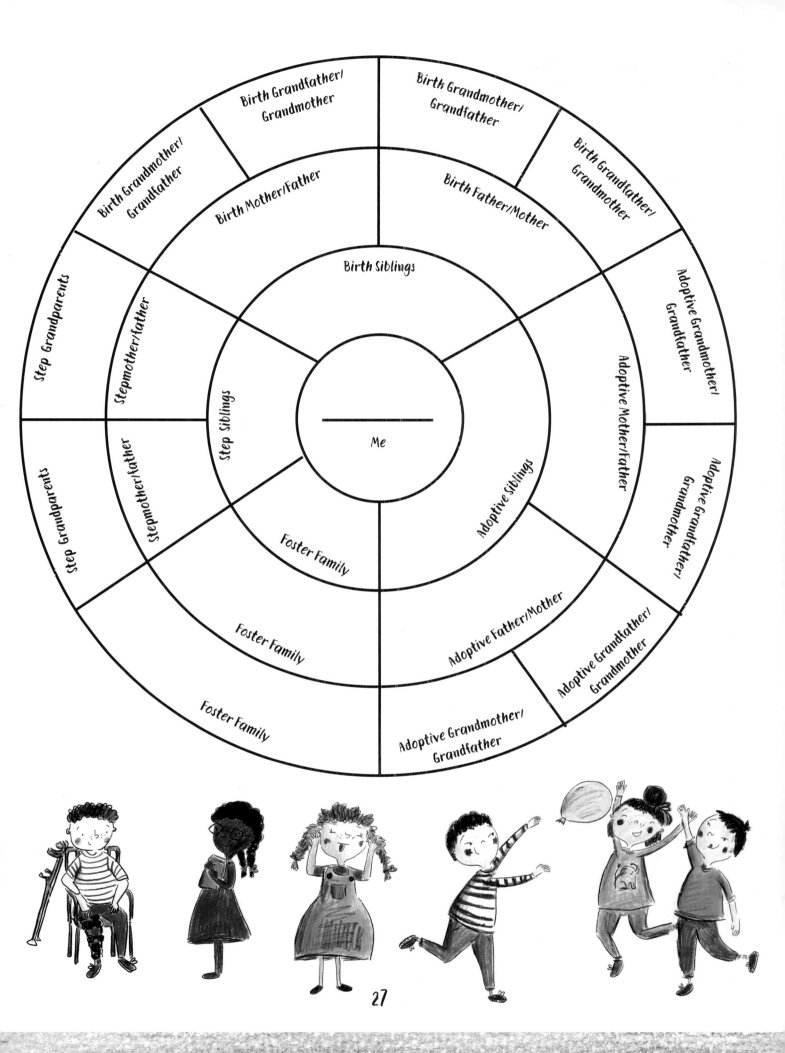

Me

Birth Siblings

Step Siblings

Foster Family

Adoptive Siblings

Birth Mother/Father

Birth Father/Mother

Stepmother/father

Stepmother/father

Foster Family

Foster Family

Adoptive Father/Mother

Adoptive Mother/Father

Birth Grandfather/Grandmother

Birth Grandmother/Grandfather

Birth Grandmother/Grandfather

Birth Grandfather/Grandmother

Step Grandparents

Step Grandparents

Adoptive Grandmother/Grandfather

Adoptive Grandfather/Grandmother

Adoptive Grandmother/Grandfather

Adoptive Grandfather/Grandmother

27

Solo parent family tree

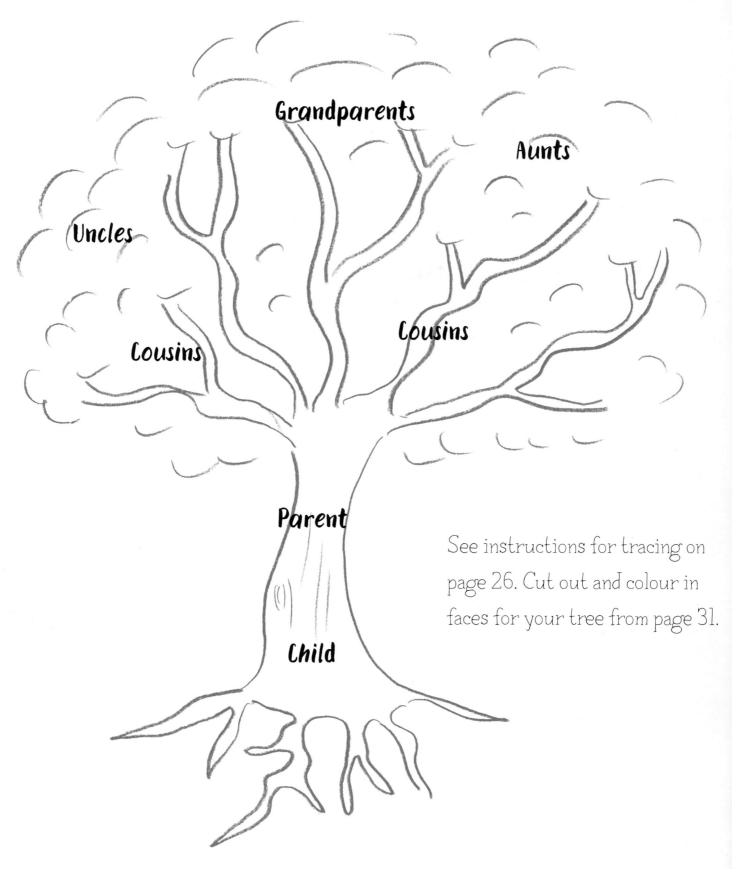

Grandparents

Aunts

Uncles

Cousins

Cousins

Parent

See instructions for tracing on page 26. Cut out and colour in faces for your tree from page 31.

Child

Tree for adopted children

Adoptive
Grandparents

Adoptive
Grandparents

Adoptive Mother

Adoptive Father

Sister/Brother

Sister/Brother

Child

See instructions for tracing on page 26. Cut out and colour in faces for your tree from page 31.

Birth Mother

Birth Father

Discovering more about your family

★ Did anyone in your family keep their school reports? They will be very interesting – and may be funny too!

★ Do any family members have any letters or papers to show how much they earned in their first jobs? Or perhaps old uniforms or pictures of themselves at work?

★ Did anyone in your family keep a diary? Perhaps of a special occasion or a family holiday?

★ If some of your family come from another part of the world, trace or photocopy a map and mark the different countries.

★ In the local library, you might find out more about the year you were born and the years your family members were born. What style of clothes did people wear? What songs did they enjoy?

★ What new things were invented? Can your teacher help you?

★ What about the place you or your family were born? Can you find old postcards of the past?

★ Ask to see old tombstones, old samplers or old family books (like someone's copy of the Bible, Quran, Torah or other books). These could help you discover even more about your family.

★ Look up books about tracing your family tree in your local library, or search online.

Cut out and colour in the members of your family tree.

Published by b small publishing ltd.

www.bsmall.co.uk

Text and illustrations copyright © b small publishing ltd. 2017

1 2 3 4 5

ISBN 978-1-911509-16-5

Design: Louise Millar   Production: Madeleine Ehm   Publisher: Sam Hutchinson   Original co-author: Tat Small

With thanks to Beth and Alex at Inclusive Minds for their inclusivity and diversity consultancy

Printed in China by WKT Co. Ltd. All rights reserved.